7 LIFE LESSONS FROM THE TRAILER PARK

WHITE TRASH WISDOM FOR EVERYONE

CLYDE A. MIDDLETON

DTS Publishing

CATONSVILLE, MD

Clyde A. Middleton/DTS Publishing

clyde@clydemiddleton.com

www.clydemiddleton.com

www.lessonsfromthetrailerpark.com

7 Life Lessons from The Trailer Park/Clyde A. Middleton

ISBN-13: 978-0-578-50721-7

DEDICATION

To my parents, Allen Spencer (Abe) and Dorothy (Dottie) Middleton, who sacrificed so much to ensure my siblings and I never wanted for the necessities and who's life lessons helped me grow and expand beyond my expectations.

To my wonderful wife, Kat, this book would not have been possible without your many years of love and support.

To my three sons, Chris, Al, and Lou, I cannot express how proud I am of you and the men you've become.

To my grandchildren, Spencer, Kathryn, Clyde and Sam, you bring pure joy to my world.

CONTENTS

ACKNOWLEDGMENTS

I want to extend a special thank you to all my Toastmasters friends that encouraged me and assisted me with this book. A very special thank you to Dominique Brightmon, Chris Jordan, and Jeff Davis for your invaluable advice and support.

PREFACE

I am, what today would be considered an endangered species. I am one of the few remaining **true** Floridians. Unlike many who call themselves Floridians, as a true Floridian, I was born and raised in Florida and someone who remembers how Florida was before Disney staked its claim.

Much of my childhood we lived in Lake Griffin Trailer Park, in Leesburg Florida along the shore of Lake Griffin. I assumed for marketing reasons and to remove negative connotations; it was renamed Lake Griffin Mobile Home Park. Some occupants of the park used the term 'mobile home' instead of a trailer. However, over time, I noticed that the homes, as well as the occupants, seldom moved.

We did move a couple of times if only to a different lot in the trailer park. I remember coming home from elementary school one day to find our single wide was replaced with a fifteen-foot-wide (a double-wide) trailer. The new trailer meant, for the first time, I had a bedroom to call my own.

My parents were good people and hard-working. We never wanted for any necessities of life. We always had a roof over our heads, shoes on our feet, heat during the winter and food on the table. I must admit there was a necessity missing: an air conditioner.

As I entered my teen years, I noticed for the first time that other families seemed to be doing a lot better than we were. Families had more beautiful houses, better cars, fancier clothes, and central air conditioning. All during my childhood, I heard my parents say, "We can't afford that" or "Do you think money grows on trees?" I began feeling sorry for myself and my life.

After others began to call me "white trash", I began to believe their words. I started to doubt my self-worth and my value to the world. I began to think I was nothing more than what people called me. Their words spoke the truth about me. I was hurting, and each day the hurt grew. It grew to the point that I believed the world would be better off without me. I got to the point where I thought suicide was the only option. So, I took the option and attempted to take my life.

Although I blocked most of that time from my memory, I do remember the hurt look of my parents' faces and the tears in their eyes. I am sure they were asking, "Where did we fail?"

During the first night back home, I remember getting up to go to the bathroom to discover that my father had made a bed for himself by pulling an old wooden sofa in front of my bedroom door. The couch was at least a couple of feet short of his six-foot frame. When I came out of my room, he asked where I was going? I told him to the bathroom. I will never forget his next words, "I'll be right here when you get back."

At that moment, I realized I was not alone. My father and mother had been there all along, and they would never leave me. I began to understand all the life lessons they had attempted to teach me and would continue to teach me; that *I am more than someone's opinion*. I am thankful and forever grateful for the life lessons they taught me.

The following lessons are the results of their sacrifice and examples, me making many mistakes, falling and getting back up, experiencing happiness and sadness, and finally realizing I am responsible for my life.

My hope is these lessons will encourage you in your life's journey.

Please visit lessonsfromthetrailerpartk.com to
download your free workbook.

If you put a small value on yourself, rest assured the world will not raise the price.

—*JOHN C. MAXWELL*

LESSON 1

GET YOUR SH*T TOGETHER

While in my teens, Dad would often remind me to get my *shit* together. He also reminded me life was not easy and not fair. He reminded me life does not give you what you want, it gives you what you deserve.

I grew up in a safe environment. Both of my parents were involved in my life. I had people in my life that cared for me. However, inside me was a deep gnawing feeling that if I did not change my direction in life, I would never amount to anything. I was desperately seeking direction for my life.

One day after work at Turner's Furniture Store, I found myself standing in front of a gray rectangular building located one block south of the store on Magnolia Street. It was a simple structure made of cinder blocks and consisting of three offices. On each of the doors were the emblems representing the Army, Navy and Marine Corps.

As I stood in front of the recruitment office for each service, I remember asking myself, "What would be the biggest challenge?" Without hesitation, I chose the Marine Corps. (I never said I was the brightest bulb in the package.) I walked into the office, letting my freak flag fly (for the young people, that's letting my long hair fly), and boldly stated, "I want to join!"

The recruiter nearly fell out of his chair. After regaining his composure, he asked my age, looked at my driver's license for verification and promptly produced the required paperwork. In a matter of minutes, I enlisted in the United States Marine Corps and would report to Paris Island Recruitment Depot, South Carolina in 90 days.

I turned to exit the building feeling immensely proud of my decision. I was walking taller with my head held higher. As I stood outside on the sidewalk, one of the consequences of my decision suddenly hit me. How was I going to tell Mom and Dad?

My opportunity came a few hours later. I was driving down Thomas Avenue taking Mom and Dad to the Safeway grocery store on West Main Street, and figured it was a good time to bring it up. I sheepishly announced, "I joined the Marines today." Mom first glanced at me and then Dad and said, "Abe, did you hear what your son said?" Without hesitation, he simply replied, "It'll do him good!" Nothing more was said.

To put this decision to join the Marine Corps in perspective, I was so desperate to change my environment; I joined during the Vietnam War. I found it more appealing to have the possibility of going to war than remaining in my current situation.

Guilty as Charged!

One of my favorite movies is the 1973 "*Papillon*" starring Steve McQueen. It's about a French criminal named Henri "The Butterfly" Charrière. He is sent to the Devil's Island penal colony where he declares his innocence and insists, he was framed. In a dream, he must defend himself before an inquisition. However, they inform him that he is not being punished for the crime that sent him to prison, but for living a worthless life. He then realizes that he is, "Guilty. Guilty. Guilty."

I was also guilty of living a worthless life.

I believe at some point in everyone's lifetime; there comes a need to change your environment to grow and become the person we were meant to be. I think that the decision to change comes from inspiration or desperation. In my case, I was extremely desperate to change my direction in life.

If we want to grow and reach our potential, we must put ourselves in the right environment. That usually requires us to make changes.

In my situation, I assumed I would automatically grow. As the years passed, I was getting taller, stronger, becoming more capable of doing new things and facing new challenges. I was developing physically, but not in my personal growth. I finally understood to change my direction in life, I had to change.

I don't know your situation. I don't know what joy, pain or regrets you have experienced in your life. However, I do know this: before you can move forward, you must forgive those you believed have wronged you and, more importantly, you must forgive yourself.

The Past Is a Canceled Check

There can be no regrets for our lives at this point. We must use our past to motivate ourselves to move forward. Remember the past is there only to inspire and teach us and others. It is a canceled check. Your past is not an indication of your future. The longer we live in the past, the more we cheat ourselves of our potential and our destiny. We must look forward and dream of what we truly want to achieve.

Dreaming is important. It inspires us. It motivates us. It's a glimpse of our possibility. But I must warn you. If we remain in a constant state of dreaming about our future and take no action, we become an unchanging dreamer. We become lost in our thoughts and forget our vision. Without action, there is no future. Without effort, our dreams are nothing more than *insignificant wishes.*

The Secret to Success

Want to know how to succeed? How you can change those dreams into reality? First, you must decide what you truly desire. Second, determine the cost you will have to pay to get it and finally, you must resolve to pay that price.

Everything we desire has a cost, and it must be paid upfront and in full.

Many people want to be a success but are not willing to pay the price. They take life for granted. They take life as it happens to them. Instead of making life happen for them. Rather than acting, they remain where they are and settle for average: average house, average car, average job, an ordinary life.

We are not here on this earth to be average. We are here to be exceptional. We have at our fingertips skills and talents to help us in overcoming life's challenges, achieving our goals and enduring whatever life has in store for us. Do not spend your life being afraid and making excuses.

Decide what you want from life, make a plan, and implement it.

You'll See It When You Believe It

You have probably heard people say or maybe you've said, "I'll believe it when I see it." They have it backward. Successful people say, "I'll see it when I believe it."

One of the most powerful steps you can take in life is to increase your belief. If you don't believe you can make a difference, you won't. No matter how gifted you are, how many opportunities you get, or how many resources you have at your disposal, you must believe. You must believe in yourself and not rely on another person's opinion of you.

*When you buy into someone's opinion of you, you
buy into their lifestyle.*

For many of my earlier years, I didn't believe I was destined to achieve anything. I thought I was inadequate and would never amount to anything. It was not until I enlisted in the Marines, took my place on the yellow footprints, and made it through boot camp that I began to believe. I found out I was mentally stronger than many of my fellow recruits. Many of which were bigger and physically stronger than my 145-pound skinny frame.

My newly found belief in myself had encouraged me when no one else did. Whether I was doing something significant or trivial, my faith in myself stayed with me when others didn't. I'm not suggesting you join the Marines to increase your belief in yourself. However, for me, it was the turning point in my life.

Believing big begins with believing in yourself. Do you believe you can make a difference? Do you believe you have a contribution to make that will positively impact the world? Or are your beliefs about yourself holding you back?

If you have never heard this before, listen to this now:

You are an incredibly powerful individual.

Start Small – But Start

It is easy to forget that people we view as successful or who achieved great things started out making small changes.

Change is difficult, but it becomes much easier when you do it a little at a time. When we attempt to make significant changes over-night, it creates within us fear, uncertainty, and resistance. We see the change as unachievable, and therefore we quit. We give up and make excuses. When we take small steps by making small changes, the difference becomes less threatening and helps us overcome our procrastination.

"Success is gained in inches at a time, not miles."
John Maxwell

Start with small changes. What can you improve by some small percentage? Can you read a book to broaden your thinking ever so slightly? Can you find a way to reorganize your desk to be more efficient? Any small change that makes you better is worth making. These small changes add up to significant improvements over time.

We all desire to be encouraged. We all love to be inspired. Nevertheless, here is a simple truth when it comes to personal growth: Motivation gets you going, but it takes discipline to keep you growing.

To become more disciplined and consistent in your personal achievement, you need to become more disciplined and consistent in your growth. How can you do that? By developing success habits and staying focused.

Develop Great Habits

Legendary NFL coach Vince Lombardi said, "Once you learn to quit, it becomes a habit." Are you in the habit of quitting? Do you regularly set a goal and quit at the first sign of resistance or difficulty?

You will never improve your life until you change something you do daily. That means being disciplined daily and forming great habits.

Discipline is the connection between goals and accomplishments, and that connection must be traversed every day. Over time that daily traverse becomes a habit. Ultimately, people do not decide their future; they decide their habits and their habits decide their fate. As an author and speaker Brian Tracy says. "From the time you get up in the morning to the time you go to sleep at night, your habits largely control the words you say, the things you do, and the ways you react and respond."

What are you doing every day that needs to change? What needs doing? Perhaps more important, what needs undoing? What are you willing to change doing today to change what you will be doing tomorrow?

"If you develop the habits of success, you'll make success a habit."
Michael Angier

In the end, hard work is really the accumulation of easy things you didn't do that you should have. It's like diet and exercise. Everyone wants to be slim, but no one wants to make the right choices to get there. It's hard work when you've neither eaten right nor exercised day after day. However, if you make small correct decisions each day, day after day, you will see results.

You can't make changes only on the days you feel in the mood. That is a guaranteed journey to failure. The secret is following through. As the founder of SuccessNet, Michael Angier says, "If you develop the habits of success, you'll make success a habit."

The Habit Poem by Anonymous

I am your constant companion.
I am your greatest helper or heaviest burden.
I will push you onward or drag you down to failure.
I am completely at your command.

Half the things you do, you might just as well turn over to me, and I will be able to do them quickly and correctly.
I am easily managed; you must merely be firm with me.
Show me exactly how you want something done, and after a few lessons, I will do it automatically.

I am the servant of all great men,
And, alas, of all failures as well.
Those who are great, I have made great.
Those who are failures, I have made failures.
I am not a machine, though I work with all the precision of a machine.
Plus, the intelligence of a man.
You may run me for profit or run me for ruin; it makes no difference to me.
Take me, train me, be firm with me and I will put the world at your feet.
Be easy with me, I will destroy you.
Who am I?
I am a HABIT!

We will discuss habits and how they are formed in more detail in Lesson 2 – Watch Your Thoughts.

Stay Focused

E. M. Gray said, "The successful person has the habit of doing the things failures don't like to do. The successful person doesn't like doing them either, but his dislike is subordinated to the strength of his purpose." The more in tuned you are to your purpose, and the more dedicated you are to proceed toward your goal, the better your chances of reaching your potential, expanding your possibilities and achieving something significant.

In the book by Gary Keller, "The One Thing", Gary asked the focusing question:

*What's the **ONE Thing** I can do such that by doing it everything else will be easier or unnecessary?*

The question is deceptively simple that the power of the question is easily dismissed by anyone who doesn't closely examine it. That would be a mistake. This simple but powerful question can lead you to answer, "big picture" questions such as, "Where am I going?" Also, it can answer "small focus" ones, "What must I do right now to achieve the big picture?"

To stay on course for the best possible day, month, year or career, you must keep asking the focusing question. When you repeatedly ask yourself the question, it requires you to line up tasks in their levered order of importance. Each time you ask it, you see the next priority. Now it's time to ask yourself, "What's the one thing I can do such that by doing it everything else will be easier or unnecessary?"

To become the person, you were created to be; you must do more than wander through life and hope everything works out for you. You need to discover what you want, plan to achieve it, and take massive action. In the words of my father, "You've got to get your Shit together."

Action Steps:

- Make a list of everything you like about personal growth. If the list is very short, work at it. Anything you can find as motivation will help you develop your growth habits.

- Make a list of *why* you want to change. Think of immediate and long-term benefits.

- Continually ask yourself the Focusing Question.

LESSON 2

WATCH YOUR THOUGHTS

If I asked you who you talked to the most in a day, who would you name? A friend. A family member. A loved one. Who?

The answer is *yourself*. Believe it or not, you have an ongoing dialog with yourself all the time. We are continually talking with ourselves. Asking and answering questions about ourselves. This internal conversation is having a profound impact on your self-esteem, and your self-esteem is the single most significant key to your behavior and ultimately your success.

One of my favorite speakers, Zig Ziglar, said, "It's impossible to consistently behave in a manner inconsistent with how we see ourselves. We can do very few things in a positive way if we feel negative about ourselves." Zig has a very practical, common sense wisdom that he has shared with people for years.

Imagine that you want to do something great in your life that impacts a lot of people. That desire, no matter how high, will be limited by your belief in yourself. If you have a desire for a 10 and your self-esteem is a 5, you will never reach the level of a 10. You will perform at your level of self-esteem or lower.

If you want to become the person you have the potential
to be, you must believe you can!

What Are You Saying to Yourself?

What is the nature of your self-talk? Do you encourage yourself? Or do you criticize yourself? If you are positive, then you are creating a positive self-image. If you are negative, you are undermining your self-worth. From where does this negative thought come? Usually from our upbringing. John Assaraf and Murray Smith, the authors of *The Answer*, write about the negative messages children receive while growing up. They wrote:

> *By the time you're seventeen years old, you've heard the words "No, you can't," an average of 150,000 times. You've heard "Yes, you can," about 5,000 times. That's thirty nos for every yes. That makes a powerful belief of "I can't."*

That is a lot to overcome. To change our lives, we must change the way we think of ourselves. To change the way we feel about ourselves, we must change the way we talk to ourselves. The older we are, the more we must take responsibility for our thoughts and how we think. Let me ask you, "Don't you have enough to deal with in life?" Why add to the problems by thinking negatively of yourself every day with negative self-talk? Several years ago, I found a poem from 1916 written by Edgar Guest. I believe it is one of the best descriptions of the danger of "can't."

Can't by Edgar Guest

Can't is the worst word that's written or spoken;
Doing more harm here than slander and lies;
On it is many a strong spirit broken,
And with it, many a good purpose die.
It springs from the lips of the thoughtless each morning

And robs us of courage we need through the day;
It rings in our ears like a timely sent warning
And laughs when we falter and fall by the way.

Can't is the father of feeble endeavor,
The parent of terror and halfhearted work;
It weakens the efforts of artisans clever,
And makes of the toiler an indolent shirk.
It poisons the soul of the man with a vision,
It stifles in infancy many a plan;
It greets honest toiling with open derision
And mocks at the hopes and the dreams of a man.

Can't is a word none should speak without blushing;
To utter it should be a symbol of shame;
Ambition and courage, it daily is crushing;
It blights a man's purpose and shortens his aim.
Despise it with all of your hatred of error;
Refuse it the lodgment it seeks in your brain;
Arm against it as a creature of terror,
And all that you dream of you someday shall gain.

Can't is the word that is foe to ambition
An enemy ambushed to shatter your will;
Its prey is forever the man with a mission
And bows but to courage and patience and skill.
Hate it, with hatred that's deep and undying,
For once it is welcomed 'twill break any man;
Whatever the goal you are seeking, keep trying
And answer this demon by saying: "I can."

While in boot camp, whenever a recruit used the word 'can't,' he was quickly reminded that "Can't means you won't in the Marine Corps!" I quickly learned to eliminate that word from my vocabulary.

Can't means you won't in the Marine Corps!

You need to learn to become your encourager, your cheerleader. Every time you do a good job, don't just let it pass; give yourself a compliment and a pat on the back. Every time you make a mistake, don't bring up everything that is wrong with yourself; tell yourself this is the price of growth and you will do better the next time. Everything you say about yourself is your reality. Ensure you are saying positive things about yourself.

Few things impact a person's self-esteem more than the way they talk with themselves daily. Are you aware of how you talk to yourself? I encourage you to keep track of how you talk to yourself. As a reminder, I have the following words printed on a business card and carry it in my wallet as a daily reminder.

Watch your thoughts for they become words.
Choose your words for they become actions.
Understand your actions for they become habits.
Study your habits for they become your character.
Develop your character for it becomes your destiny.

If you study the words, you will see the progression to your destiny. It all starts with your thoughts. I encourage you to ask your close friends or family members to tell you whether they think you view yourself in a favorable or unfavorable light.

The Unlimited Power of Our Mind

What separates us from all other life forms on this earth? The answer is simple: The mind. We were given a powerful instrument that can take us to extraordinary heights and unbelievable feats. The problem is it didn't come with an owner's manual.

We can divide the mind into two parts: conscious mind and subconscious mind. The conscious mind is the portion you think with, your free will, and your imagination. The conscious mind can accept, reject, or neglect any idea received from our five senses or our thoughts.

The subconscious mind is the part where we react to life, our long-term memory, our values, and our belief systems are all stored here. In short, it is where our self-image resides. It cannot reject or neglect. It can only accept an idea.

A senior biologist, Bruce Lipton, estimated that the conscious mind works around 2,000 bits per second. This is extremely impressive; except when it is compared to the subconscious mind. The subconscious mind operates at 4,000,000 bits per second. It operates all the complex systems of our body.

We don't have to consciously think about making our heartbeat, digesting our food, taking a breath, maintaining our body temperature, cell replacement and oxygenating our blood. These systems and more are operated by our subconscious mind without us needing to think about it. The subconscious mind knows no limits except the limits we consciously choose.

We can choose to focus on all significant accomplishments, all the challenges that we overcame, and all our successes. On the other hand, like most people, we can choose to focus on our shortcomings, all our disappointments, our failures, and the things we should have done. Just because we failed at something does not make me or you a failure.

Every thought your conscious mind chooses to accept,
the subconscious mind must accept.

Most people are programmed to allow their conscious mind to be occupied by news and events outside of themselves and their control. They often allow the opinions of others to shape their thinking or allow the negativity of the media to flood their consciousness. They fail to realize none of it is an accurate reflection of the world we live in. Most people are unaware of what they are subjecting themselves too. I certainly did, and it drove me to attempt suicide.

Once you understand the difference between the conscious and subconscious mind, you will know that no person or circumstance can cause you to think thoughts or ideas that you did not choose. You become aware that you, and only you, are responsible for our outcomes in life. In the classic book *Think and Grow Rich*, Napoleon Hill states, "We have complete control over the material which reaches our subconscious mind through our five senses." There is a measure of freedom in that knowledge.

"We have complete control over the material which reaches our subconscious mind through our five senses."
Napoleon Hill

Let's Revisit Habits

When we first attempt to learn a new skill or activity, we must concentrate on the task. We must continuously think about our actions. We are using a lot of brain power. After a while of replication, the task becomes easier. We begin thinking less of the steps involved in the task. It becomes an unconscious thought. It becomes a routine.

The process in which the brain converts a sequence of actions into an automatic routine is known as "chunking," and it's at the root of how habits form. Currently, there are hundreds, if not thousands, of these chunks that we rely on every day. Some are simple. You don't have to think about how to open a door. You don't have to relearn how to walk each day. Some, like getting dressed or preparing a meal, are a little more complicated.

Others are so complicated, and it is amazing how little effort is required to accomplish such complicated tasks. I want you to think about when you first started to learn to drive. Take the task of backing the car out of the driveway. It involved unlocking the car door, adjusting the seat and mirrors, inserting the key in the ignition, turning it clockwise, checking for obstacles, applying the brakes, shifting into reverse, removing your foot from the brake pedal, placing your foot on the accelerator, adjusting the amount of pressure to safely move the car, turning the steering wheel to safely navigate obstacles, checking for other traffic and pedestrians, and countless other tasks you must perform.

Now you do all that every time you get in your car with hardly a thought. The routine, the series of actions, has become a habit.

Scientists believe habits emerge because the brain is continually looking for ways to save energy. The brain, left unchecked, will try to make almost any routine into a habit, because habits allow our minds to ramp down more often to conserve energy.

The Habit Loop

In the book, *The Power of Habit*, by Charles Duhigg, he discusses a three-step loop within our brain when it comes to habits. First, there is a *cue*, a trigger that tells our brain to go into automatic mode and which habit to use. The next step, which can be physical, mental, or emotional, is called the *routine*. The last step is the *reward*. This final step helps our brain figure out if the chosen habit is worth keeping for the future.

As time passes, this loop – cue, routine, reward – becomes more and more automatic. It becomes intertwined until a powerful sense of anticipation and craving emerges. A habit is born.

Habits can be ignored, changed, or replaced. There is a fundamental truth to the habit loop; When a habit emerges, the brain stops fully participating in decision making. It stops working so hard or diverts focus to another task. If you don't fight a habit and find a new routine, the pattern will unfold automatically.

The good news is now that you understand how habits works, it makes them easier to control.

Habits don't disappear. They become encoded in our brains, and that is a significant advantage for us. Can you imagine the necessity of needing to relearn how to drive each day? As discussed early, the problem is that our brain cannot tell the difference between good and bad habits. So, if we have a bad one, it will always be lurking there, waiting for the right cue and rewards.

This explains why it's so hard to create a new habit, such as exercising. Once we develop a routine of sitting on the couch, rather than running, this pattern always remains inside our brain. The good news is we can create new patterns that will replace the old patterns. Studies have shown, going for a run instead of sitting on the couch becomes automatic as any other habit.

Habits are critical. Without them our brains would shut down, overwhelmed by the trivial details of daily life. However, the brain's dependency on automatic routines can be dangerous. Habits can be a curse as much as a blessing.

Anger Is a Habit

Do you find yourself responding to specific situations with anger? For example, do you find yourself instantly getting angry when another driver cuts you off? Now that you understand how habits work, you know that it has become an automatic response. You did not consciously decide to become angry; you just do. Your angry reaction became a habit. To change your response, you must identify the trigger and your reward. Once you have accomplished this, you can implement a new routine.

You must continually evaluate your habits. Are your habits taking you closer to your dream or are they leading you away from it? What habits do you need to change to achieve your dream?

Study your habits for they become your character.

Unfortunately, there is no specific set of steps that will guarantee to change a habit. Each person is different. What works for one person, may not work for another. If we keep the same trigger and the same reward, a new routine can be inserted.

However, that is not enough. For you to form a new habit and for it to stick, you must believe change is possible. Most often, that belief only comes with the help of a group. Identify what habit you want to change, believe you can change it, and find a support group (It can be a group of two; yourself and a friend) to help you stay on course.

Action Steps:

- Are you aware of how you talk to yourself? Maintain a record of how many times each day you say something positive or negative about yourself.

- Make a list of all your best personal qualities. If you have positive self-esteem, then this will most likely be easy for you. If you don't, it may be a struggle. Spend time compiling the list.

- Read the list each day to remind yourself of your value.

- Repeat to yourself 50 times daily, "I love myself."

- Eliminate the word *can't* from your vocabulary.

- If you want to improve your attitude, don't listen to the news for a week.

- Take a break from social media. If a "friend" constantly posts negative information, unfollow them.

LESSON 3

NO ONE LIKES A WHINER

My father would often tell me, "Stop your whining. No one likes a whiner." I don't know what part of the country you are from, but in my family that translated to, "Do I need to give you a whoopin'?" It was a warning to "get my mind right and stop my whining."

One of the definitions of a whiner is: "a person who complains or expresses disappointment or unhappiness repeatedly." As I matured, it became apparent to me that my whining was nothing more than an outward indication of my attitude. I began to understand that people's attitude toward me depended greatly on my attitude toward them and my attitude gives me happiness. In short, I am totally responsible for my attitude.

Is it possible for someone with a bad attitude to have success? The answer is yes, but their attitude will determine how much they enjoy their success.

I understand, life happens, and things occur that are out of our control. However, there is something that is completely within our power to control: *our attitude*. The way we respond to the pressures of life is entirely in our control.

Instead of getting annoyed when that driver cuts you off, smile and wish them a safe journey. I guarantee you they will not think of you the entire day.

Instead of angrily blaming the boss when you get overlooked for a promotion, ask for feedback on why and then work to improve in the suggested areas.

Instead of grumbling at your coworkers after you woke up on the wrong side of the bed, ask them if there is something you can do for them.

It's easy to allow ourselves to play the victim of circumstances. It's easier to blame other people, the weather, the teachers, the government, the economy or fill-in-the-blank, for our lousy mood, hurt feelings, and cynical outlook on life. But that is a victim's mindset. You give up your power when you succumb to big or small problems life throws at you. You take back your power by merely choosing to view it differently and then responding accordingly. I came across a humorous prayer that I thought reflected my struggle each morning. It reads:

> *Dear Lord,*
>
> *So far today, I am doing alright. I have not gossiped, lost my temper, been greedy, grumpy, nasty, selfish, or self-indulgent. I have not whined, cursed, or eaten any chocolate.*
>
> *However, I am going to get out of bed in a few minutes, and I will need a lot more help after that.*
>
> *Amen*

It will not always be easy to keep a good attitude, but if you try hard enough, you can find something beneficial, even during challenging situations. Mother Theresa was asked the requirements for people assisting in her work with the destitute in Calcutta. She stated two things: the desire to work hard and a joyful attitude. If someone could be expected to be joyful among the dying and the poorest of the poor, then surely, we can do the same in our situation.

We need to start being more accountable for how we show up. The world is in desperate need of positivity. Our attitude has a profound effect on us and those around us. It is entirely up to us how positive or negative that impact will be. What will you choose?

Bad Experiences Can Be Blessings

We often do not remember the things that make us who we are, but they did happen. Whether they were positive or negative, we now live the results.

I had a ninth-grade teacher, who will remain nameless, that drove me crazy. I remember only two things about him; Getting my first failing grade and memorizing a poem.

That year I had broken my right arm playing murderball (a somewhat severe form of four-corner dodgeball). I struggled to work on an essay assignment using my non-dominate left hand. After several hours of writing with my left hand, I completed the task and proudly handed it in for grading. I was shocked to find the nameless teacher gave me an 'F.' Written below the grade was the simple word, "Unreadable."

The other assignment that year, he made us memorize a poem, which at the time seemed to me like a monumental task. We had to deliver the poem in front of the class to pass the course. I made it because I got a diploma, but I don't remember my performance.

The poem was "IF" by Rudyard Kipling. As you read the poem, imagine the good it has subconsciously done for me over the years.

If by Rudyard Kipling

If you can keep your head when all about you
Are losing theirs and blaming it on you;

If you can trust yourself when all men doubt you,
  But make allowance for their doubting too;
If you can wait and not be tired by waiting,
  Or being lied about, don't deal in lies,
  Or being hated, don't give way to hating,
  And yet don't look too good, nor talk too wise;

If you can dream—and not make dreams your master;
  If you can think—and not make thoughts your aim;
If you can meet with Triumph and Disaster
  And treat those two impostors just the same;
If you can bear to hear the truth you've spoken
  Twisted by knaves to make a trap for fools,
  Or watch the things you gave your life to, broken,
  And stoop and build 'em up with worn-out tool;

If you can make one heap of all your winnings
  And risk it on one turn of pitch-and-toss,
  And lose, and start again at your beginnings
  And never breathe a word about your loss;
If you can force your heart and nerve and sinew
  To serve your turn long after they are gone,
  And so, hold on when there is nothing in you
  Except the Will which says to them: 'Hold on!'

If you can talk with crowds and keep your virtue,
  Or walk with Kings—nor lose the common touch,
If neither foes nor loving friends can hurt you,
  If all men count with you, but none too much;

If you can fill the unforgiving minute
With sixty seconds' worth of distance run,
Yours is the Earth and everything that's in it,
And—which is more—
You'll be a Man, my son!

I remember how much I despised the teacher for giving me an 'F' for penmanship and requiring me to memorize the poem. However, I am glad for the experience. Not necessarily for the failing grade, but for introducing me to Kipling's poem. It has made a positive impact on my attitude and ultimately my life.

Eliminate Negative Words

One of the best techniques to improve your attitude and ultimately your life is to improve your vocabulary by eliminating negative words from your dialog. Substitute the words 'I can't' with 'I can.' Quit using the words 'I'm afraid' and substitute them with 'I'm fearless.'

If you will continually look for and embrace the positive and eliminate the negative, you will begin thinking more positively each day.

Focus on Your Strengths

Each of us has our own set of strengths or gifts. However, we tend to compare our weakness against someone else's strength. Comparing yourself to others is just an unnecessary distraction. The only person you need to compare yourself with is you. Our purpose is to become better today than we were yesterday.

Focus on what you can do better today to improve yourself. If you do this enough, the progress you make over weeks, months, and years will surprise you.

Be Grateful Daily

Gratitude seems to be the least virtue that is expressed. How often do you go out of your way to thank someone? How often do you write a thank you note? When you get out of bed in the morning, is your attitude of dread for what the day may hold? When people ask me how my day is going, I respond with, "I woke up this morning above ground, and that's a good start." In this era of plenty, we tend to take things for granted.

Thinking about the positive aspects of our lives, helps us be grateful. The fact you woke up this morning on the green side of the grass, is a blessing and another chance to live up to your potential. Remaining grateful helps us to have a positive attitude.

Your Attitude Requires Constant Adjustment

Like any other discipline, your attitude requires constant monitoring and adjustment. Each day you need to monitor your attitude and look for any warning signs your attitude might be in trouble.

Remember, you are in complete control of your attitude.

Action Steps:

- Read the poem daily; memorize it if you like. It will transform your attitude upward at light speed.

- Take an inventory of how often you use negative words in your conversation and begin to replace them with positive words.

- Make a list of things in your life for which you are grateful. No matter the circumstances of your current situation, there is always something to be thankful for.

LESSON 4

TODAY IS A GIFT

We are probably the only creatures on this earth that understand we are going to die; that our time here on earth is finite. However, for many of us, we waste this precious gift of today.

Each of us has 24 hours in a day and seven days in a week. That is a total of 168 hours given to us and everyone else. How we choose to use the time is what makes the difference between being successful or unsuccessful, rich or poor.

I thought I had all the time in the world. I often said, "I'll do it tomorrow." I believed that until July 31, 2004, when life taught me a harsh lesson.

It was a day my wife Kat, and I were looking forward to with great anticipation and excitement. We were driving in the Corvette heading up to Philadelphia to see Cirque du Soleil's *Alegrìa* under the Grand Chapiteau. We had seen portions of the show on the Bravo television channel, and we were looking forward to seeing the live performance.

Since we had purchased a VIP package, we were able to park the car in a reserved parking section located a short walk from the main entrance. As we made our way through the opening, we transported to another world. Kat and I looked at each other, and we both realized this was not going to be like anything we had seen before. This was not going to be your typical circus.

We found our seats located just a few rows from the stage and waited for the show to begin. Before the show started, various clowns were out entertaining the audience. We avoided eye contact with them for fear of becoming part of the entertainment.

The lights soon dimmed, the band began playing, and the tent filled with an angelic voice singing the main song *Alegría*. We were like two kids again and knew we were in for a special night.

The first act barely completed before my cell phone began to ring. I retrieved the phone from my pocket. The call was from a number I did not recognize. However, I did know the area code 352 meant the call was from central Florida. Probably someone from my hometown. You need to remember this was before the use of caller id, texting and voice mail. You had to depend on knowing the caller by the phone number. Yes...those were primitive times.

With the music playing and not wanting to disturb my fellow audience members by going to the lobby, I decided not to answer the phone and wait for intermission to return the call.

We could not wipe the smiles from our faces as we watched. Acrobats performing high flying tricks on two separate trapezes. A group of entertainers performing flips and twist on an X-shaped power track. Incredible feats of hand balancing and contortionist passing their body through hula hoops.

Throughout the performances, my phone continued to ring, and each time it did, I ignored it.

Following each act, the troupe of clowns entertained the audience. The final act before the intermission was called *Snowstorm*. It is an iconic clown act created by Slava Polunin and today performed by Yuri Medvedev.

You may have guessed by the name there may be some snow and wind involved. You would be correct. The act contained a full-on blizzard finale which immersed the audience with high winds and paper slivers as snow. The snow was falling on every part of the Grand Chapiteau. It drifted on the aisles and the floor — what a glorious spectacle.

As the lights in the Grand Chapiteau rose and the final reminisce of the snow floated to the floor, I reached into my pocket to retrieve my phone and return the call from the mysterious person. Little did I realize that the past performance would be a forecast of what awaited me on the other end of that phone call.

I dialed the number and my youngest brother, Darrell answered it. I said, "What's up?"

I could tell by the tone of his voice something was wrong. His next words instantly drained the joy of the evening. I hung up and immediately turned, looked at Kat and said: "We have to go!"

Without any further explanation, I rapidly turned and began heading for the exit. Kat followed close behind and had no clue as to what news was just shared by my brother.

As I walked toward the car, I vaguely remember hearing her behind me repeatedly saying "What's wrong? What's wrong?" I didn't answer. I was still processing what Darrell had told me. I look back on it now and think what a selfish jerk I was to her.

The next thing I remember was sitting in the car. As my mind began to process the news, I returned to the present and heard Kat asking, "Clyde, what's wrong?" Barely holding back the tears, I turned to face her and said, "Mom died."

The 90-minute drive back to our home in Catonsville done in silence. My mind filled with thoughts of what needed accomplishing. How do we get to Leesburg? Do we fly or drive? What arrangements needed making? What caused her death? What about Dad? What in the hell happened?

Hundreds of thoughts raced through my head. None of them truly important. I was letting my mind wander over unnecessary items, so I could not face the fact: *I will never get the opportunity to talk to her again.*

All the things I should have said but never seemed to have the time, now gone. Always saying, "I'll do it tomorrow." There will never be another opportunity to tell her. She was gone. I had missed my chance to tell her everything I meant to say to her.

Nothing Is Accomplished Alone

None of us can claim we have accomplished anything on our own. We must remember that anything we have achieved; we did not do it alone. There are always others who helped us reach our dream. We need others, and we need to let them know it.

I know it sounds like an old cliché, but we are not guaranteed tomorrow. Take time to think about who has helped you in your life. Who brings out the best in you? Who are you grateful for being in your life?

When you start having a greater appreciation of other people, it will inspire you to get outside of yourself and put others first. If you think about it, others have often put you first over themselves.

Before it's too late, you must let these people know how much you appreciate what they've done for you. Don't put yourself in the position I found myself with the death of my mother. Don't put it off until tomorrow. Let them know **NOW** how much they mean to you.

I'm Time... I'm a gift... and you're wasting it.

The movie *Collateral Beauty* starring Will Smith, Edward Norton, Kate Winslet, Michael Peña, Jacob Latimore, and Helen

Mirren again drove the importance of time home for me. It is a story about a man, after experiencing a tremendous personal loss, begins to question the universe by writing letters to Love, Time, and Death. To his surprise, they answered him.

Two lines from the movie stirred me the greatest. The first is when Brigitte, Helen Mirren representing Death, is talking to Simon, Michael Peña, who discovered he is dying from cancer.

Brigitte: Death is so much more vital than Time.

Simon: Right.

Brigitte: Death gives Time all of its value.

The second line, we should all take to heart and remember each day we wake up. It was expressed by Jacob Latimore, who represented Time, to Claire, Kate Winslet.

Raffi: Remember me... I'm Time... I'm a gift... and you're wasting it.

Do It Now!

This day is a gift. Are you living it to the fullest? With purpose and passion? Are you pursuing your dreams or are you distracted? Are you seizing the day or is the day seizing you? There are times, everybody puts things off until the last minute. We have all procrastinated some time or another. How many times did you put off things today?

You probably have said to yourself, "I perform better under pressure." I've said it, but most of the time it was my way of justifying putting things off. Do you find saying to yourself, "It's not the right time" or "I don't feel like doing it now, I'll do it tomorrow." The problem is tomorrow may never arrive. Life is flying by. This is your one and only shot. We don't get a do-over. We can't relive any of our past. Once today is over, we can never get it back.

In the *Law of Diminishing Intent*, John Maxwell states, "The longer you wait to do something you should do now, the greater the odds that you will never actually do it." To develop ourselves, we must shift from the habit of I'll do it later to the mindset of I'll do it now.

Decide today that you are going to begin living each day with intention. Set your goals and be disciplined in sticking with it. Decide you will not waste another day. Ensure that you are investing your time and not wasting it. If you do this, I guarantee, the seeds of greatness inside you are going to take root and begin to flourish.

Today is a gift. Don't waste it.

Action Steps:

- Write down a minimum of 10 names of individuals who have enriched your life.

- Next to each name, write down how they enriched your life.

- Set a date and time you will meet them, write them a letter, or call them (no texting or email) and tell them how much you appreciate how they enriched your life. If they are no longer with us, write the letter, read it out loud, and then burn it.

- For the next 30 days straight, each evening before going to bed repeat to yourself 50 times, "Do it now!" And each morning, repeat the phrase "Do it now!" 50 times. If you miss a day, start the 30 days over.

LESSON 5

THE WORLD DOESN'T SPIN AROUND YOU!

O ne day my father took me to a family friend's house to rake leaves. If you ever lived In Florida, you realize that we do have a fall season. The time of the year when all the oak trees drop their leaves. Of course, not at the same time but spanning several weeks. It is an excellent opportunity to make extra money.

We arrived at Bea's house, a lady in her seventies, and as I prepared to start raking, my father informed me I needed to remove the leaves under the house. Bea's house was raised about two feet above the ground, and the leaves blew under the house and accumulated a couple of inches deep.

To accomplish this task, I was required to crawl under the house and rake the leaves from a prone position. In other words, on my belly. Between the spider webs, dust, dirt, and leaves I was having a great time. All the time I was thinking, you are going to owe me for this.

After hours of raking, I emerged from under the house covered from head to toe in dirt. I was ready for my reward for all my hard work. I held out my dirt-covered hand and awaited my payment. With great pride, Bea dropped two shining quarters in my hand. To say I was disappointed is an understatement. I worked hours crawling on my belly raking leaves, and I received payment of 50 cents. Dad said thank you, I mumbled an insincere thank you, and we got back in the truck to head home.

On the way back, Dad noticed I was not thrilled about my payment. He looked at me and said, "What's the matter?"

I replied in anger, "I crawled on my belly, worked for hours, and all I got was 50 cents!"

He replied, "Maybe that's all she had. To her, it was a great deal of money."

At the time, his response did not ease my disappointment. However, it gave me another outlook of the world. It's not about what we get, but what we give to others that truly counts. I later discovered that Bea was on a fixed income and money was tight. She could not afford to have other individuals come and do the work.

Every few weeks, there was something that needed repair at her house. Some repair work to the house my father would do and use it as an opportunity to teach me how. I continued to rake leaves for her every year until her passing — my payment, the joy of helping someone who needed help and whatever she deemed appropriate compensation. From that moment onward, I was always grateful for whatever she gave me.

The Golden Rule

Each morning Benjamin Franklin asked himself, "What good will I do today?" and each evening, "What good have I done today?"

These questions are powerful because it causes you to focus on what needs to be done. It made me realize that I could become more intentional in my ability to help others and keep myself accountable for it daily. As I've grown older, that has changed from being merely a good idea to becoming my greatest desire.

"The golden rule is the very foundation of all the
better qualities of man."
Napoleon Hill

I've discovered that the way you treat people has an enormous impact on your life. You probably heard of the Golden Rule. The most familiar version of the rule says, "Do unto others as you would have them do unto you." This principle of treating others as one's self wishes to be treated, appears prominently in Buddhism, Christianity, Hinduism, Islam, Judaism, Taoism, and many of the world's major religions.

"If you help people get what they want, they will help you get
what you want."
Zig Ziglar

I embrace the simplicity of the Golden Rule. You apply it to all your interactions with different people when:

- You help your neighbors.

- You treat your family with kindness.

- You take the time to encourage your coworkers.

- You assist a stranger in need.

Besides helping the other person, you will soon realize people will begin treating you better. As the inspirational speaker and author, Zig Ziglar, said, "If you help people get what they want, they will help you get what you want."

That is a pretty good deal.

Decide to Serve Others

To serve others, you must develop yourself first. People can sense your attitude toward them. They know when you look down on them or want to raise them higher. They know whether you are in it for yourself or truly building them to achieve higher goals. That's why serving others must begin in our hearts.

Do you genuinely care about people and want to help them be their best? Do you want them to succeed at least as much as you want yourself to succeed? Most of us are selfish, including me. We all must work at developing our willingness to serve.

You must have the spirit to serve others. You must have an attitude of gratitude. You must wake up each morning thinking about how you can help people succeed in their personal and professional life. If you make people better or more successful in any way, you're on the right track.

Each day we must endeavor to develop the heart of a servant and show our growth through our actions.

"How far you go in life depends on your being tender with the young, compassionate with the aged, sympathetic with the striving and tolerant of the weak and strong. Because someday in your life you will have been all of these."
George Washington Carver

Ray Hansell captures the sentiments made by Mr. Carver in his poem, *Make A Difference*.

Make A Difference by Ray Hansell

Make a difference
Each day you live.
Open your heart
Learn to give.

Life for many
Is so unkind
Giving people
Are hard to find

So open your heart
Give what you can
We're all responsible
For our fellow man

It's so easy to look
The other way
But the tables could turn
On any given day

So help if you can
For one day you may be
The one who's down and out
The one no one will see

The Good Samaritan

Someone asked Jesus, "Who is my neighbor?" He shared a story about a Jewish man traveling from Jerusalem to Jericho who was robbed, beaten, and abandoned for dead on the side of the road. Two people, a priest and a Levite, passed by without offering any help. However, the third man from Samaria came to his aid. An essential aspect of the story to remember is that Samaritans and Jews were enemies in those times.

The Samaritan treated the man's wounds and took him to a hotel where he cared for him. Before leaving, the Samaritan gave the innkeeper money and promised to return to check on the injured man.

After telling the story, Jesus asked His listeners to identify the true neighbor among the three men who came upon the beaten man. When someone responded that it was the Samaritan because he alone had mercy on the victim. Jesus said, "Go and do likewise."

As I close out this lesson, I want to encourage you to "go and do likewise." No matter your theological beliefs, I encourage you to develop empathy for others, as the good Samaritan showed. Do everything you can to protect others from emotional and physical harm.

What good will you do today?

Action Steps:

- Each morning and evening, ask yourself Benjamin Franklin's questions:

  - What good will I do today?

  - What good have I done today?

- Identify what you can work on that will help you serve people better.

- Identify where you can add value to someone.

- Ask yourself, "What is it like for people to work with me?"

7LIFE LESSONS FROM THE TRAILER PARK • 51

LESSON 6

YOU BECOME WHO YOU HANG OUT WITH

My dad had many rules for living under his roof and eating the food he provided that my mother lovingly prepared. But one of them is the subject of this chapter. The first unbreakable rule: Never wear a hat in the house. NEVER! The second rule: He and mom required they meet every one of our friends, and they are obligated to respect rule number one.

Many of the people I brought to the house passed his critical eye. However, at times my father's critique of someone was filled with rather colorful expressions. He wanted to ensure I was not hanging out with "damn idiots." He understood that the people I surround myself with would have a significant influence on the person I would become.

According to Dr. David McClelland, a research social psychologist of Harvard, the people with who we habitually associate are called our "reference group," and these people determine as much as 95 percent of our success or failure in life.

One of my favorite speakers and business philosopher, Jim Rohn, asserted that we become the combined average of the five people we hang around the most. Mr. Rohn would say we could tell the quality of our health, attitude, and income by looking at the people around us. He believed that we begin to eat what they eat, talk like they talk, read the same material, think the same, watch the same shows, and dress as they dress.

Who are the people closest to you? Are they lifting you or holding you back? Whether we accept it or not, our lives are influenced by those surrounding us. That influence is either positive or negative.

"Surround yourself with people who are going to lift you higher."
Oprah Winfrey

Are You Proud of What You Are Becoming?

It is your choice who you decide with whom and how you spend your days. Your time is valuable, don't waste it engaging in consistent daily failure. Look at the people who you associate with daily. Would you like to exchange places with them? Are they adding value to your life? Are their values aligned with yours?

Friends play an essential role in our life. Understand, there is nothing wrong with spending time with friends now and then. However, if you spend a great deal of your time with friends with bad attitudes, no purpose, no dreams, and no ambition to succeed in life, you need to understand the impact their beliefs will have on you. You must reduce the time you spend with them.

It is not about abandoning your friends. It's about focusing on your success and becoming the best person you can become. You can always return later to share your growth experiences and offer your assistance with their growth. However, in the beginning, you must stop wasting significant time engaging in minor activities with average people.

Are you satisfied with what you are becoming or have become? Take a moment to evaluate, which direction is your life heading. Slipping into the life of someone else is easy. It seems as though it is just the way people live. They want you to come into their world. They want you to do what they do. They want you to become like them. It is not intentional. It's just the way they have been living.

Don't let people pull you into the life of mediocrity. You must understand, your growth is a reminder to them of what they could have been.

People will tell you all the reasons you cannot succeed. They will make subtle suggestions that cause you to doubt yourself, give-up, or to quit before you even start. These dream stealers have the attitude 'that's a bad idea,' or 'that won't work.' These are the people who have never done anything, yet they are experts on everything. They want to hold you back and stop you from becoming who you dream of becoming. Why? Because you might prove to be a little better than them. They are going to try and steal your dream because they don't have a dream of their own.

Don't let someone who gave up on their dreams
talk you out of yours.

Your Mastermind Group

The Mastermind Group is a mentoring concept through which individuals can form groups to learn from each other and grow together.

Napoleon Hill first introduced the concept of Mastermind Groups in his book Think and Grow Rich (1937). In the book, he described Mastermind as a group of at least two people who come together to solve problems.

"No two minds ever come together without thereby creating a
third, invisible intangible force, which may be likened to a third
mind [The master mind]."
Napoleon Hill

The value of the Mastermind Group is that members elevate the bar by challenging each other to create and realize goals, brainstorm ideas, and support each other with honesty, respect, and compassion.

If you want to become a millionaire, you will not team together or get much help if everyone surrounding you is making the same amount of money as you. I know what you are thinking, "I don't know any millionaires." That may be true. However, many successful people in all walks of life have written books about their successes, and more importantly about their failures.

Find someone who has achieved where you want to be and ask them to be in your mentoring group. You may be asking yourself, "Why would someone earning more than me and more successful than I want to be part of my Mastermind Group?" The answer is simple: many successful people who have reached the top of their field want to be involved with helping others who are genuinely striving to become more.

You need to surround yourself with people who lift you instead of knocking you down — people who are striving towards making the world a better place, people we can learn from, and those inspired to achieve greatness.

The most significant factor in our environment are the people who surround us. If you change nothing else in your life for the better than that, you will increase your chances for success.

We must surround ourselves with individuals who are pushing the limits and living life on their terms. You can only improve your life if you surround yourself with winners.

Action Steps:

- List the names of your "reference group". Next to each name write what that person contributes. Do they lift you up or drag you down?

- Start a Mastermind Group. (Sample guidelines can be found in the workbook at lessonsfromthetrailerpark.com)

  - Identify the subject of the Mastermind Group.

  - Identify and invite 4-8 people you want in your mastermind group.

  - Setup a date, time, and frequency of your Mastermind Group.

LESSON 7

WHO SAID LIFE WAS FAIR?

I believed at the time that making it through the 13 weeks of training at Parris Island would be my toughest challenge in life. I thought after enduring the physical and mental obstacles placed in my path to becoming a Marine; it would prepare me for anything life could throw at me. I could not have been more wrong.

My mother's sudden death indeed threw me for a loop, and in my heart, I knew that dad would soon follow. However, I was not prepared for what ensued. Life was about to show me how unfair it can be.

Over the next few months following mom's death, Kat and I would travel to Leesburg to check on him. On each visit, we noticed that his health and zest for life was waning. He was missing his Dottie. A woman he was married to nearly 60 years, raised seven children with and together built a loving home for all of us.

With each visit, it was becoming more evident to us; he could not and did not want to continue living without her. He had done his part. He had created a family and provided them with everything needed to survive in this world. He stopped taking care of himself. He stopped caring for his basic daily needs: properly eating, taking a shower. At one point my brother Terry had to fight him to get him into the shower. He had lost his will to live. His wife buried below the ground under a mound of soil while he is buried above ground in a mound of grief.

Sometimes Doing the Right Thing Still Hurts

One of the toughest decisions I would ever make is when I came to the realization; I needed to place him in a nursing home — a place he never wanted to be.

Kat and I searched and found a beautiful facility that would take great care of him. No matter how much I justified this was the correct thing to do, it did not lessen the pain. I was taking away dad's freedom, removing him from his home and placing him in a place he never wanted to go, and likely, die there.

As the staff was preparing Dad for his stay, I had to excuse myself. Seeing him so helpless and void of life, caused my heart and spirit to hit the lowest point of my life. I stepped into the hallway and leaned my back against the wall. I slid down the wall as the weight of the events pushed me to my knees. Placing my hands over my face, I began uncontrollably crying. I had not shed that many tears in years.

Each time Kat and I would visit him, he would beg me to take him home. Each time I had to tell him that it was not an option; it was best for him. Every time I saw the hurt in his eyes. Each time I relived the pain of that moment when I first placed him in the nursing home.

Cause of Death – Broken Heart

Friday morning as I prepared to fly down and visit Dad, I called to check on how he was doing and if he needed anything. When the staff member answered the phone, I asked to be connected to Allen Middleton. She responded by saying, "Hold for a moment." She returned several minutes later and said, "Mr. Middleton, I must tell you your father passed away last night."

I don't remember what I said in response, but I was instantly saddened and relieved at the same time. My only thought was Dad had gone home to be with his true love.

The medical examiner reported the case of death as a Massive MI. However, I believe he died from a broken heart. His heart could no longer take the strain of being away from her. He missed his Dottie.

We All Experience Pain

Life is hard, but it's hard for everyone. We all experience pain in our lives. We all had terrible experiences. There is one thing for sure; no one likes them while we are going through them. It's just downright painful. Nobody escapes bad experiences.

We will do anything within our power to avoid painful experiences. It doesn't matter how much we try; they have a way of finding us. It does not matter if we are good people, what we do for a living, what neighborhood we live in, or how rich or poor we are, we all must deal with adversity. Author Dennis Wholey observed, "Expecting the world to treat you fairly just because you're a good person is a little like expecting the bull not to charge you because you are a vegetarian." There is an undeniable truth; you can't avoid them.

"Expecting the world to treat you fairly just because you're a good person is a little like expecting the bull not to charge you because you are a vegetarian."
Dennis Wholey

Pain is Personal

No one's pain is more significant than someone else's pain. What pain I have endured may seem trivial to what you may have experienced. And what pain you've experienced may not seem that difficult to me. It does not matter. It hurts.

John Maxwell asserts in his book, *The 15 Invaluable Laws of Growth*; everyone has a pain file. A pain file of events that had or are still having a dramatic impact on their lives and how they respond to it. What distinguishes the difference between successful and unsuccessful people, is how they handle these experiences.

Besides the death of my parents, I've had my share of failures. Here are just a few of mine:

- The pain of braces during high school.

- The pain of two divorces.

- The pain of lost relationships.

- The pain of missing my sons growing up.

I want to be upfront and honest with you. I want you to understand you will experience the pain of lost relationships. As you strive to reach your potential, you will soon discover you will separate from friends who have no desire to grow with you.

Life is filled with good and bad experiences and some of it we can't control. As we discussed in Lesson 3, our attitude has a lot to do with how we respond to adversity. If we have a positive attitude, the good or bad will become better. If we have a negative outlook, the good and bad will become worse.

Learn from Your Pain

If you are like me, you've probably heard the expression, "Experience is the best teacher." I found the statement to be false. It turns out "Evaluated experience is the best teacher." If we don't take time to learn from the bad experiences that occur in our life, we are doomed to repeat them, and the next time, it may cost more, and the pain caused may be higher.

"Strength and growth come only through continuous effort and struggle."
Napoleon Hill

When bad experiences create strong feelings in us, we either face the feelings and try to change, or we try to escape. It's the old fight-or-flight instinct. We need to prepare ourselves to fight for positive changes. How we respond to adversity has a significant impact on our lives.

The next time you find yourself in a painful circumstance, remind yourself that you are about to have the opportunity to change and grow. You need to take a long-term view of life rather than being caught up in the turmoil of the past. We must teach ourselves how to stop worrying and begin living.

Stop Worrying

Learn to love and respect yourself. Be proud of yourself and for the person you have become or are becoming. You don't need to explain yourself or make excuses to anyone else.

The best way to stay relaxed in the face of life's ups and downs is to decide to forgive anyone who has hurt you in any way. Keep your attention focused on the future and where you are going. The only impact the past has on you is the impact you allow. When you forgive someone who hurt you, you do not necessarily forgive them of their actions. You forgive them so that you can move forward.

Another way to stop worrying and start living is to take life one day at a time. Forget what has happened in the past. The past cannot be changed.

Mother Theresa captured this philosophy best when she said: "Yesterday is gone. Tomorrow has not yet come. We have only today. Let us begin."

Nothing in your history is an indication of your future.

No matter what you have gone through or currently going through in your life, you have the opportunity to grow from it. I understand it is challenging to see opportunity in the middle of the pain, but it is there. You must pursue it.

"Yesterday is gone. Tomorrow has not yet come. We
have only today. Let us begin."
Mother Theresa

Action Steps:

- Make a list of your painful experiences.

- Identify what you learned from each of the experiences.

- Make a list of people you believe have wronged you.

- Forgive those who wronged you and especially yourself.

- Now destroy the list.

RECOMMENDATIONS

"The greatest gift you can give somebody is your own personal development."
Jim Rohn

Join a Local Toastmasters Club

Toastmasters International is a non-profit educational organization that teaches public speaking and leadership skills through a worldwide network of clubs. Headquartered in Englewood, Colorado, the organization's membership exceeds 357,000 in more than 16,600 clubs in 143 countries. Since 1924, Toastmasters International has helped people from diverse background become more confident speakers, communicators, and leaders.

I advise you to visit several clubs before deciding which one to join. Every club has a unique personality. Find one that meets your growth requirements.

Go to www.toastmasters.org to find a club near you.

Leaders Are Readers

Get in the habit of reading. Invest in yourself. If you can't afford the books, get a library card.

"You will be the same person in five years as you are today with the exception of the people you meet and the books you read."
Charlie "Tremendous" Jones

A University of Southern California study revealed that if you live in a metropolitan area and drive 12,000 miles a year, you can acquire the equivalent of two years of college education in three years by listening to educational information in your car. The average American adult spends two hundred to seven hundred hours each year in an automobile. Take advantage of it. Become a member of Automobile University.

Set a goal of reading or listen to one book a week for the next year. Below is a list of suggested books.

1. *As a Man Thinketh — James Allen*
2. *Failing Forward — John C. Maxwell*
3. *The Magic of Thinking Big — David Schwartz*
4. *The One Thing — Gary Keller*
5. *Maximum Achievement — Brian Tracy*
6. *First Things First — Steven Cove*
7. *Winning with People — John C. Maxwell*
8. *Keys to Success — Napoleon Hill*
9. *NLP: The Essential Guide — Tom Hoobyar, Tom Dotz, and Susan Sanders.*
10. *Leading an Inspired Life — Jim John*
11. *Leadership — Rudolph W. Giuliani*
12. *Never Eat Alone — Keith Ferrazzi*
13. *Brain Rules — John Medina*
14. *The 7 Habits of Highly Effective People — Stephen Covey*

15. *Think and Grow Rich — Napoleon Hill*

16. *7 Strategies for Wealth & Happiness — Jim Rohn*

17. *Man's Search for Meaning — Victor Frankl*

18. *The Richest Man in Babylon — George S. Clason*

19. *How to Win Friends and Influence People — Dale Carnegie*

20. *The 21 Irrefutable Laws of Leadership — John C. Maxwell*

21. *The Power of the Subconscious Mind — Joseph Murphy*

22. *Dig Your Well Before You Are Thirsty — Harvey Mackay*

23. *Intentional Living — John C. Maxwell*

24. *It's Not Over Until You Win — Les Brown*

25. *Leaders Eat Last — Simon Sinek*

26. *The Science of Getting Rich — Wallace D. Wattles*

27. *The Power of Habit — Charles Duhigg*

28. *The Magic of Thinking Big — David J. Schwartz*

29. *Wooden: A Lifetime of Observations and Reflections On and Off the Court — John Wooden*

30. *Drive — Daniel H. Pink*

31. *The Five Major Pieces to the Life Puzzle — Jim Rohn*

32. *Eat That Frog — Brian Tracy*

33. *Good to Great — Jim Collins*

34. *Secrets of the Millionaire Mind — T. Harv Eker*

35. *The Power of Focus — Jack Canfield, Mark Victor Hansen, Les Hewitt*

36. *You Can't Steal Second with Your Foot on First! — Burke Hedges*

37. *How Full Is Your Bucket — Tom Rath and Donald O. Clifton*

38. *The 12 Essential Laws for Becoming Indispensable — Dr. Tony Zeiss*

39. *The Message of You — Judy Carter*

40. *Create Your Own Future — Brian Tracy*

41. *Put Your Dreams to The Test — John C. Maxwell*

42. *Reach Your Mountaintop — Jeff Davis*

43. *Your Roadmap for Success — John C. Maxwell*

44. *The Gifts of Imperfection — Brenè Brown*
45. *Aspire — Kevin Hall*
46. *Making Ideas Happen — Scott Belsky*
47. *No Limits - John C. Maxwell*
48. *Focal Point - Brian Tracy*
49. *Who Moved My Cheese — Spencer Johnson*
50. *How to Talk to Anyone —Leil Lowndes*
51. *A Game Plan for Life: The Power of Mentoring — John Wooden*
52. *Influence: The Psychology of Persuasion — Robert B. Cialdini*

ABOUT THE AUTHOR

Clyde Middleton is a John Maxwell Team Certified Coach, Teacher, and Speaker. Clyde is passionate about personal growth and leadership development and has been for over 25 years. He brings a unique mix of talent and experience that shaped his philosophy and view of the world.

He is passionate about inspiring and equipping individuals to value themselves and others, by developing and maintaining a positive self-image, showing compassion to others, persevering amid adversity, and creating a daily routine of successful attitudes and behavior. In 2009, he was named the Speaker of the Year by the Maryland Business Roundtable for Education.

Since July 2005, Clyde is an active member of Toastmasters International and earned the highest educational award of Distinguished Toastmaster. He served as an award-winning Club president, Area, and Division Director, Club Growth Director, Program Quality Director and Select Distinguished District 18 Director of Toastmasters International.

Facebook: Clyde.Middleton.5

LinkedIn: ClydeMiddleton

Email: Clyde@ClydeMiddleton.com

Website: www.clydemiddleton.com

Website: www.lessonsfromthetrailerpark.com

Made in the USA
Columbia, SC
01 March 2021